A CourseGuide for

Four Portraits, One Jesus

Mark Strauss

ZONDERVAN
ACADEMIC

ZONDERVAN ACADEMIC

A CourseGuide for Four Portraits, One Jesus

Copyright © 2019 by Zondervan

ISBN 978-0-310-11112-2 (softcover)

Requests for information should be addressed to:
Zondervan, *3900 Sparks Dr. SE, Grand Rapids, Michigan 49546*

All Scripture quotations, unless otherwise indicated, are taken from The Holy Bible, New International Version®, NIV®. Copyright © 1973, 1978, 1984, 2011 by Biblica, Inc.®
Used by permission of Zondervan. All rights reserved worldwide. www.Zondervan.com.
The "NIV" and "New International Version" are trademarks registered in the United
States Patent and Trademark Office by Biblica, Inc.®

Any internet addresses (websites, blogs, etc.) and telephone numbers in this book are
offered as a resource. They are not intended in any way to be or imply an endorsement
by Zondervan, nor does Zondervan vouch for the content of these sites and numbers
for the life of this book.

No part of this publication may be reproduced, stored in a retrieval system, or trans-
mitted in any form or by any means—electronic, mechanical, photocopy, recording, or
any other—except for brief quotations in printed reviews, without the prior permission of the publisher.

Printed in the United States of America

CONTENTS

Introduction

Welcome to *A CourseGuide for Four Portraits, One Jesus*. These guides were created for formal and informal students alike who want to engage deeper in biblical, theological, or ministry studies. We hope this guide will provide an opportunity for you to grow not only in your understanding, but also in your faith.

How to Use This Guide

This guide is meant to be used in conjunction with the book *Four Portraits, One Jesus* and its corresponding videos, *Four Portraits, One Jesus Video Lectures*. After you have read each chapter in the book and watched the accompanying video lesson, the materials in this guide will help you review and assess what you have learned. Application-oriented questions are included as well. For additional practice, you will want to complete exercises found in *Four Portraits, One Jesus Workbook*.

Each CourseGuide has been individually designed to best equip you in your studies, but in general, you can expect the following components. Most CourseGuides begin every chapter with a "You Should Know" section, which highlights key terminology, people, and facts to remember. This section serves as a helpful summary for directing your studies. Reflection questions, typically two to three per chapter, prompt you to summarize key points you've learned. Discussion questions invite you to an even deeper level of engagement. Finally, most chapters will end with a short quiz to test your retention. You can find the answer key to each quiz at the bottom of the page following it.

For Further Study

CourseGuides accompany books and videos from some of the world's
top biblical and theological scholars. They may be used independently,
or in small groups or classrooms, offering quality instruction to
equip students for academic and ministry pursuits. If you would like
to engage in further study with Zondervan's CourseGuides, the full
lineup may be viewed online. After completing your studies with *A
CourseGuide for Four Portraits, One Jesus*, we recommend moving on to
A CourseGuide for How to Read the Bible for All Its Worth and *A Course-
Guide for Thinking Through Paul*.

CHAPTER 1

What Are the Gospels?

You Should Know

- The four Gospels were written to provide four unique portraits of Jesus Christ.

- The Synoptic Gospels have many common stories and similar language. The Gospel of John provides a different style, much unique material, and a more theological presentation.

- The Gospel genre may be identified as *historical narrative motivated by theological concerns*. Each Gospel writer had a particular purpose in writing and particular themes to develop.

- The Gospels were written with reference to the needs and concerns of particular communities within the church, but also with an eye toward their wider distribution among all the first-century churches.

- The Gospels are best read "vertically," following each narrative through the plot from beginning to end. The Holy Spirit inspired four distinct Gospels with their own unique themes and purposes.

- Reading the Gospels "horizontally"—comparing their accounts to one another—enables the reader to see more clearly each Gospel's particular themes and theology.

- Harmonizing the Gospels into a single story risks distorting each Gospel writer's unique contribution. Harmonizing is helpful, however, when seeking to answer historical questions about the life of Jesus.

- Greco-Roman sources outside the New Testament provide very little additional information concerning the historical Jesus.

- The so-called apocryphal gospels may contain an occasional authentic tradition about Jesus, but are generally late and unreliable accounts, far removed from the historical events.

- Synoptic Gospels: Matthew, Mark, and Luke

Reflection Questions

1. Why do we have four Gospels instead of one?

2. What are the Synoptic Gospels and how do they differ from John's Gospel?

3. Describe the Gospel genre and its various characteristics.

Essay Question

1. What does it mean to read the Gospels "vertically" or "horizontally"? Include the benefits.

Quiz

1. (T/F) The apocryphal gospels provide a great deal of early and reliable information concerning the historical Jesus.

2. (T/F) The text argues that the Gospels are best read and studied harmonistically, bringing them together as a single story.

3. (T/F) The Gospels have much in common with Greco-Roman works known as *bio*, or biographies.

4. (T/F) The *implied audience* refers to the general kinds of readers of the Gospels.

5. (T/F) According to the text, the Gospels were primarily written to unbelievers.

6. The early Christian writer who tried to merge the four Gospels into a single harmony, or *Diatessaron*, was named:

a) Augustine
b) Tatian
c) Papias
d) Luther

7. To read the Gospels "horizontally" means:

   a) To follow each story through from beginning to end
   b) To compare the Gospels to one another to discern their distinctives
   c) To examine the historical contexts and background of each Gospel
   d) To search for the sources behind each Gospel

8. To read the Gospels "vertically" means:

   a) To compare the Gospels to one another to discern their distinctives
   b) To search for the sources behind each Gospel
   c) To examine the historical contexts and background to each Gospel
   d) To follow each story through from beginning to end

9. The apostle Paul uses the term "gospel" (*euangelion*) to describe

   a) The oral preaching of the good news about Jesus
   b) The Gospel of Mark
   c) The Gospel of Luke
   d) The Gospel of John

10. The Jewish historian _____ briefly mentions Jesus twice in his writings.

   a) Caiaphas
   b) Augustine
   c) Josephus
   d) Hillel

CHAPTER 2

Exploring the Origin and Nature of the Gospels

Historical-Critical Methods of Gospel Research

You Should Know

- The message of Jesus was originally passed down primarily by word-of-mouth, gradually being written down to produce our current four Gospels. Historical criticism examines this process with methods such as form, source, and redaction criticism.

- Source criticism seeks to identify and evaluate the written sources used by the Gospel writers.

- The synoptic problem is the question of the literary relationship between Matthew, Mark, Luke, and the Synoptic Gospels. The most widely held view is that Mark wrote first (Markan priority) and that Matthew and Luke used Mark and other sources.

- The designation "Q" is used for the "double tradition," the common source or sources used by Matthew and Luke in addition to Mark. The designations "M" (Matthew's special source) and "L" (Luke's special source) are used for the unique material each utilized.

- A minority of scholars hold to the priority of Matthew (the Griesbach hypothesis). A few claim the Gospel writers wrote independently, using only common oral traditions.

- Form criticism seeks to identify and evaluate the oral (spoken) forms of the stories about Jesus, which lie behind our written sources. Form critics in general have rejected much of the historicity of the Jesus tradition, attributing its creation to the early church.

- Redaction criticism seeks to evaluate the process by which the Evangelists redacted, or edited, their sources to produce the Gospels. Redaction critics try to discern the main themes and theology of each Gospel writer, and to establish the *Sitz im Leben* ("setting in life"), the community situation in which the Gospel arose.

- Mark has a larger number of "difficult" and potentially offensive readings than the other two Synoptics.

- A short episode (pericope) which climaxes in an authoritative statement by Jesus is called a pronouncement story

- A "redactor": an editor

Reflection Questions

1. What is the synoptic problem and the most widely held solution?

2. What is source criticism? What are its goals?

3. What is form criticism? What are its goals?

Essay Question

1. Summarize the four stages that led to the production of the Gospels.

Quiz

1. (T/F) Form criticism studies the final editing of the sources by the Gospel writers.

2. (T/F) Source criticism studies the nature of the written sources behind our written Gospels.

3. (T/F) Redaction criticism studies the "oral period" of the transmission of the Gospel tradition.

4. (T/F) Stage 1 in the period of development of the Gospels was the period of oral tradition, when the sayings and stories of Jesus were passed down primarily through the spoken word.

5. (T/F) According to the text, the *synoptic problem* is that the Gospel of John has more different stories than do the other three Gospels.

6. Which early church father first discussed a potential literary relationship among the Synoptic Gospels?

    a) Jerome
    b) Augustine
    c) Tertullian
    d) Polycarp

7. Which Gospel is considered to have been written first by most NT scholars?

    a) Matthew
    b) Mark
    c) Luke
    d) John

8. The designation "Q" refers to gospel material:

    a) That appears in Matthew and Mark, but not in Luke
    b) That appears in Matthew and Luke, but not in Mark
    c) That appears in Mark and Luke, but not in Matthew
    d) That does not appear in any current Gospel

9. The Two (or Four) Source theory says:

    a) Matthew wrote first, and both Luke and Mark used him as a source
    b) Mark wrote first, and both Matthew and Luke used him as a source
    c) Luke wrote first, and Mark and Matthew both used him as a source
    d) Matthew wrote first, and Mark wrote independently of him

10. The Griesbach Hypothesis claims that:

a) Mark wrote first, and both Matthew and Luke used him as a source
b) Matthew wrote first, Luke used Matthew, and Mark used both
c) Luke wrote first, and both Matthew and Mark abbreviated him
d) There is no direct literary dependence among the Synoptics

CHAPTER 3

Reading and Hearing the Gospel Stories

Literary-Critical Methods of Gospel Research

You Should Know

- Literary criticism refers to various methods which study the Gospels as unified wholes, rather than from the perspective of sources and composition history.

- Narrative criticism examines the Gospels as story, analyzing features such as plot, character, and setting.

- The Evaluative point of view is the worldview, beliefs, and values which the implied reader is expected to adopt. The Gospels affirm the evaluative point of view of God, and of his agent Jesus Christ.

- The plot of a narrative is the progress of the story. It is made up of *events*, *scenes*, and *acts*, which move forward through *causation* and *conflict* to *climax* and *resolution*.

- Rhetorical criticism uses categories developed in the ancient world to evaluate the rhetorical methods used to produce a desired effect on the readers.

- Canon criticism seeks to read the Bible with reference to its role as inspired Scripture within the life of the church.

- Structuralism seeks to identify conventional patterns—a "deep structure"—which lies behind the surface structure of the Gospel narratives. Structuralists seek an objective analysis of the text through the identification of universal and stereotypical features of plot, character, and setting.

- Reader-Response criticism is *post-structuralist* in that it claims the meaning of the text is not to be found in its formal structure, but in the response of its readers. Reader-focused approaches are diverse, from those who claim texts have no inherent meaning and that the reader alone creates the meaning, to those who accept an original authorial meaning, but seek to discern how certain readers would hear the text.

- Liberationist and feminist approaches seek to read the text from the perspective of those who are less-empowered or oppressed within society.

- Deconstruction rejects any inherent meaning in the text, considering all language to be a means of power and oppression.

Reflection Questions

1. What is the difference between historical and literary criticism? What is the goal of narrative criticism?

2. What is the difference between a real author, an implied author, and a narrator?

3. What does "evaluative point of view" mean and how does it apply to the Gospels?

Essay Question

1. Describe the main features of plot, characterization, and setting.

Quiz

1. (T/F) Setting refers not only to places, but also to social and temporal settings.

2. (T/F) According to the text, the narrative world of the Gospels is limited to daily life at the beginning of the first century.

3. (T/F) Two fundamental features of plot are causation and conflict.

4. (T/F) The implied reader's response to the narrative is unpredictable and sometimes inappropriate.

5. (T/F) Canon criticism falls under the category of literary criticism.

6. In narrative criticism, the "implied reader" is:
   a) The historical readers who first heard the book read
   b) The "voice" you hear telling the story
   c) A present-day reader who is fully aware of the historical context of the book
   d) An imaginary person who responds appropriately to the narrative strategy

7. A "flat" character is:
   a) The villain or antagonist of a story
   b) A simple, predictable character with few complex traits
   c) A minor character who appears only once or twice
   d) The protagonist or hero of the story

8. Chiasm refers to:
   a) Any non-literal figure of speech
   b) A framing structure that "sandwiches" one story in the middle of another
   c) Inverse parallelism, such as an ABBA pattern of text
   d) A parable or similitude

9. Intercalation refers to:
   a) Any non-literal figure of speech
   b) A framing structure that "sandwiches" one story in the middle of another
   c) Inverse parallelism, such as an ABBA pattern of text
   d) A parable or similitude

10. A method that uses ancient categories developed by Aristotle, Cicero, and others is called:

a) Structuralism
b) Canon criticism
c) Narrative criticism
d) Rhetorical criticism

CHAPTER 4

The Historical Setting of the Gospels

You Should Know

- The Second Temple (or intertestamental) period of Israel's history—running from approximately the fifth century BC to the end of the first century AD—provides the historical background for Jesus and the Gospels.

- The conquests of Alexander the Great in the third century BC resulted in the spread of Greek language and culture (Hellenization) throughout the Mediterranean region.

- Antiochus IV "Epiphanes," ruler of the Syrian dynasty of the Seleucids, persecuted the Jews and tried to force Hellenization on them.

- Led by Judas Maccabeus ("the hammer") and his brothers, the "Maccabees" defeated the Syrians and gained independence for the Jews. Hanukkah is the celebration of this victory.

- The Hasmonean (Maccabean) dynasty ruled in Israel for the next seventy years, until the Roman conquest in 63 BC.

- Caesar Augustus (Octavian) was the emperor at Jesus's birth. Tiberius Caesar was the emperor during his public ministry.

- The Romans made Herod ("the Great"), an Idumean, king of the Jews. Herod was a cruel but effective ruler and a great builder. He restored and expanded the Jerusalem temple into one of the great buildings of the ancient world. Herod died shortly after Jesus's birth.

- When Herod's son Archelaus ruled Judea poorly, the emperor appointed Roman governors to succeed him. One of these governors was Pontius Pilate, who ordered Jesus's crucifixion.

- After years of unrest, the Jews revolted in AD 66. The Romans crushed the rebellion and in AD 70 destroyed Jerusalem and the temple.

- Sixty-two years later, the Jews rebelled again under Simon bar Koseba. The so-called Bar Kokhba revolt was again aggressively put down by the Romans, this time ending Israel's existence as a political state.

Reflection Questions

1. What is Hellenization? How did the conquests of Alexander the Great result in widespread Hellenization?

2. From where did the Pharisees, Sadducees, and Essenes emerge?

3. How did the *Pax Romana* help the spread of Christianity?

Essay Question

1. Summarize (briefly) the main events of the history of Israel from the close of the Old Testament to the destruction of the Jewish state in AD 135. How did the Jewish revolt of AD 66–74 change the face of Judaism and what effect did it have on Christianity?

Quiz

1. (T/F) The leader, nicknamed "Maccabeus," who became leader of the Maccabean revolt after the death of his father Mattathias was John Hyrcanus.

2. (T/F) The Seleucid period is primarily known for the tolerance shown to Jewish culture and religion.

3. (T/F) Following the conquests of Alexander the Great, Greek became the language of the common people in Palestine.

4. (T/F) The LXX became the Bible of Diaspora Jews.

5. (T/F) The Second Temple was destroyed by the Romans in 73 AD.

6. The most important influence of Alexander the Great for New Testament background is:
   a) His conquest of the Medo-Persian Empire
   b) The process of Hellenization that he initiated
   c) His fulfillment of the prophecy of Daniel 8
   d) None of the above

7. The desecration of the Temple, or "abomination of desecration," which prompted the Maccabean Revolt, was committed by:
   a) Antiochus IV "Epiphanes"
   b) Pompey
   c) Alexander the Great
   d) Ptolemy III

8. Herod was known as "the Great" primarily because
   a) He was really good at killing people
   b) He won many great military victories
   c) He was a great builder
   d) He married well

9. Herod's son _____ ruled in Judea after him, but was replaced by Roman governors because of misrule.
   a) Herod Antipas
   b) Archelaus
   c) Philip
   d) Herod Agrippa

10. The second Jewish revolt of AD 132 was led by:
   a) Akiba
   b) Simon bar Koseba
   c) Johanan ben Zakkai
   d) Hadrian

ANSWER KEY
1. F, 2. F, 3. F, 4. T, 5. F, 6. B, 7. A, 8. C, 9. A, 10. B

CHAPTER 5

The Religious Setting

First Century Judaism

You Should Know

- Core beliefs of Judaism included monotheism (Yahweh as the one true God), the covenant at Mount Sinai as the establishment of Israel's relationship with Yahweh, and obedience to the law as the means to maintain this covenant relationship.

- The two main religious institutions of Judaism were the (one) temple in Jerusalem, with its system of priests offering sacrifices, and (many) local synagogues scattered throughout the empire. Synagogues were community meeting places centered on education and the study of the law (Torah).

- Levites and priests, led by the high priest, oversaw temple worship. The Sanhedrin, or Jewish high court, was the highest religious authority in Judaism.

- Scribes were experts in Mosaic law. As synagogue worship and the study of Torah became more central to Israel's religious life, the office of scribe increased in prominence.

- The Sadducees appear to have arisen from the priestly and aristocratic families who supported the Hasmonean dynasty. They were the party of the status quo and were religiously conservative, viewing only the Pentateuch (Genesis through Deuteronomy) as fully authoritative.

- The primary opponents to the Sadducees were the Pharisees, who probably arose from the *Hasidim* who fought with the Maccabees for Jewish independence. The Pharisees viewed not only the

Hebrew Scriptures as authoritative, but also the oral traditions passed down from the fathers.

- The Essenes shared many beliefs with the Pharisees, but were even more legalistic and separatistic, often living in monastic communities (like Qumran), and holding strong end-times expectations that God would soon come to judge the Romans and the wicked leaders of Israel.

- Apocalypticism was a Jewish movement which looked to God's soon intervention to destroy the wicked, deliver the righteous, and establish God's just rule in a new age of peace and security. Apocalyptic literature was normally written in times of national crisis, when God's people were severely persecuted.

- Messianic expectations were diverse in first century Judaism, although the most widespread hope was for a Messiah from the line of David who would restore God's kingdom.

- Jewish literature providing helpful and informative background for the Gospels includes the works of Josephus and Philo, the Apocrypha and the pseudepigrapha (writings of Second Temple Judaism), and the post-biblical rabbinic writings.

Reflection Questions

1. What core beliefs did almost all Jews share? What role did the temple play in Israel's national life?

2. What were the basic beliefs of the Pharisees and the Sadducees and which group's beliefs continued to thrive after the destruction of Jerusalem and the temple?

3. What were the primary messianic expectations of first century Israel?

Essay Question

1. Who were the Essenes, Zealots, and Herodians and what did each wish to achieve? Offer a brief summary.

Quiz

1. (T/F) Most people in Israel were members of the Pharisees, the Sadducees, or the Herodians.

2. (T/F) The Zealots were a part of the group who held out against the Romans at Masada.

3. (T/F) The Targum is an Aramaic paraphrase of the Hebrew Scriptures.

4. (T/F) The Sadducees arose from the supporters of the Hasmonean priesthood.

5. (T/F) The Essenes were "lawyers," or experts in the Mosaic law.

6. The apocalyptic movement in Judaism emphasized that:
   a) God would soon intervene supernaturally on earth to save his people
   b) God's kingdom would be established progressively on earth by God's people
   c) The new age of salvation had already begun in the hearts of God's people
   d) None of the above

7. The most common and widespread messianic hope among first century Jews was for a:
   a) Prophet like Moses
   b) Davidic Messiah
   c) Priestly Messiah
   d) Son of Man

8. They probably established the Qumran community that produced the Dead Sea Scrolls.
   a) Zealots
   b) Sadducees
   c) Pharisees
   d) Essenes

9. The oldest part of the Talmud, it was put into writing around AD 200:

a) Mishnah
b) Haggadah
c) Targum
d) Halakah

10. Intertestamental literature written under an assumed name, generally later than the Apocrypha.

a) Talmud
b) Tosephta
c) Pseudepigrapha
d) Mishnah

CHAPTER 6

The Social and Cultural Setting of the Gospels

You Should Know

- The extended family was the most important social unit in the ancient world. Families were generally patriarchal, with the male head of the house exercising most authority. A woman's honor in the family came primarily through childbearing and her domestic skills.

- Marriages were generally arranged with families of similar social and cultural status. Weddings were among the most important social events in society.

- Slavery was common in the Roman Empire, although the status and privilege of slaves varied enormously. While some first-century Christians kept slaves, the New Testament provides clear indications of the evil of slavery and the need for its abolition.

- Banquets were not just meals or social events, but rituals of social status which demonstrated one's position in the community.

- Cities were larger municipalities typically surrounded by a wall. Cities were often surrounded by small agrarian villages, whose inhabitants would enter the city for protection in time of war.

- Greco-Roman cities often had many municipal facilities, including theatres, stadiums, baths, gymnasiums, and temples. Synagogues, scattered throughout the Roman Empire, were the center of Jewish community life.

- The vast majority of people were poor farmers and tradespeople.

A small upper class wielded most of the power and controlled most of the wealth.

- Upper-class Greeks and Romans considered manual labor degrading, while Jews viewed it as more honorable, and most rabbis practiced a trade.

- The most common agricultural activities of Israel and the Mediterranean region were raising livestock, fishing, and growing wheat, barley, olives, grapes, figs, and dates.

- Greco-Roman entertainment included arena games, theatre plays, athletic contests, and visiting public baths and gymnasiums. Jewish life centered more on family and the annual pilgrim festivals in Jerusalem.

Reflection Questions

1. What was the nature of first-century family life, marriages, and weddings?

2. What is the difference between group and individual mentality and which was most valued in first-century culture?

3. What do we mean by the first-century social values of honor and shame?

Essay Question

1. Social values in the first-century Middle East were sometimes very different than those of Western culture today. What were those values, and how do they differ from those of our own culture?

Quiz

1. (T/F) Marriages were generally arranged by parents in first-century culture.

2. (T/F) Slavery was very common in the Roman world, and as much as a third of the population were slaves.

3. (T/F) Most people in the Roman Empire were from the "middle class."

4. (T/F) Social status was less rigid in the ancient Mediterranean world than in Western society, and people commonly moved up and down the social ladder.

5. (T/F) In the first century, democratic values of equality and equal rights were common.

6. Families in the Greco-Roman world of the first century were generally:

   a) Patriarchal
   b) Matriarchal
   c) Egalitarian
   d) Complementarian

7. The most important agricultural products of first-century Israel were:

   a) Oranges and lemons
   b) Grapes and olives
   c) Potatoes and carrots
   d) Figs and dates

8. A walking journey from Galilee to Jerusalem took about:

   a) Twelve hours
   b) Two days
   c) Five days
   d) Ten days

9. The definition of dyadism is:

   a) A person's identity comes from being a member of a family, community, or nation
   b) Hospitality for strangers
   c) The practice of exposing babies that are not wanted
   d) The breaking of an engagement contract

10. Which of the following was NOT a characteristic of Greek and Roman men:

    a) Short hair
    b) Leather sandals
    c) Linen or cotton tunics
    d) Beards

CHAPTER 7

Mark

The Gospel of the Suffering Son of God

You Should Know

- Literary devices common in Mark include the topical ordering of events, intercalation, triads, and irony.

- The first half of Mark's Gospel presents Jesus as the mighty and powerful Son of God, defeating the forces of Satan, healing the sick, and teaching with great authority. The people respond with amazement and awe.

- Jesus's authority is also seen in spiritual conflicts, as he casts out demons and challenges the religious leaders for their hypocrisy, obsession with external rules, and failure to share God's heart for the lost.

- The turning point of the narrative comes with Peter's confession that Jesus is the Christ, and Jesus's subsequent revelation that the Messiah must suffer and die.

- Jesus's entrance into Jerusalem and his actions in the temple serve as a public announcement of his messiahship, ending the messianic secret and leading to a series of conflicts with the religious leaders. Jesus repeatedly confounds them with his superior wisdom, and they in turn plot his death.

- Jesus's arrest and crucifixion in Mark are scenes of betrayal, desertion, and rejection. The disciples flee at his arrest; his opponents mock and scorn him. He dies in agony on the cross, forsaken by all, even his Father in heaven.

- The vindication of Jesus's claims is the resurrection. The earliest and best manuscripts conclude the Gospel at 16:8. The last part may have been lost, but more likely emphasizes the *announcement* of Jesus's resurrection over narrated appearances. The reader is called to faith in the proclamation of salvation achieved through Jesus the Messiah.

- As the protagonist and main character, Jesus is portrayed in Mark's Gospel as the mighty Son of God, who suffers and dies as the Servant of the Lord—a ransom for sinners.

- Key theological themes of Mark's Gospel include the in-breaking power of the kingdom of God; the identity of Jesus as Son of God, Servant-Messiah, and suffering Son of Man; and the need for cross-bearing discipleship.

- The book was likely written for a variety of reasons, but especially to provide an authoritative written version of the oral proclamation of the gospel, to clarify the identity of Jesus as the servant-Messiah, and to call the persecuted church to faithfully follow him through suffering to glory.

Reflection Questions

1. Describe the three cycles of passion predictions and responses. What verse serves as a key theme verse for Mark's Gospel?

2. What is allegorized in the parable of the wicked tenant farmers? What does each character represent? To which Old Testament passage does this parable allude?

3. Summarize how Jesus's identity is gradually revealed in Mark's Gospel.

Essay Question

1. Summarize the main theological themes of Mark's Gospel including describing the nature of the kingdom of God.

Quiz

1. (T/F) If Mark's narrative comment in Mark 13:14 ("let the reader understand") is a reference to the outbreak of the Jewish War, then Mark probably wrote his Gospel in the late 60s of the first century.

2. (T/F) Jesus's first conflicts in Mark's Gospel are with Satan and his demons.

3. Jesus predicts his death four times in Mark's Gospel.

4. (T/F) The key midpoint and turning point in Mark's Gospel is Peter's confession and Jesus's first prediction of his death.

5. (T/F) For its length, Mark's Gospel has fewer miracles than the other three Gospels.

6. (T/F) In the shorter ending to Mark's Gospel (ending at 16:8), the disciples are vindicated and restored to fellowship with Jesus.

7. (T/F) According to the textbook, the longer ending of Mark's Gospel (Mark 16:9–20) is probably not authentic.

8. (T/F) Jesus repeatedly tells those he heals to keep silent that he is the Messiah.

9. (T/F) The tone of the crucifixion scene in Mark is one of victory and triumphalism.

10. Which of the following is an important literary feature of Mark's Gospel?

    a) Strict chronological order
    b) Very refined Greek literary style
    c) Groups of three, or triads
    d) All of the above

CHAPTER 8

Matthew
The Gospel of the Messiah

You Should Know

- Matthew's Gospel is the most Jewish of the four Gospels, presenting Jesus as the Jewish Messiah who brings God's people salvation from their sins. It is also the most systematically arranged, utilizing concise style, fulfillment formulas, topical arrangement, and structural signals to provide a carefully structured presentation.

- Matthew includes five major discourses by Jesus, and alternates between narrative and discourse, presenting Jesus as the great Moses-like bringer of the new covenant.

- Matthew's genealogy presents Jesus as the fulfillment of the covenants made to Abraham and David, and as the legitimate king of Israel.

- Jesus's healing and preaching ministry in Galilee demonstrates the power of the kingdom in his ministry to Israel and reveals the beginning of opposition from Israel's religious leaders (4:12–11:1). The Sermon on the Mount (*First Discourse*; chs. 5–7) represents Jesus's inaugural kingdom address, presenting standards of righteousness for the new covenant age of salvation. The *Second Discourse* (ch. 10) is a commissioning sermon to Jesus's disciples to take the message of the kingdom to Israel.

- At Jesus's trial and crucifixion, the religious leaders continue to act treacherously against Jesus; the disciples desert him; Pilate fails to exercise justice; and the fickle crowds call for his crucifixion. Yet Jesus remains in control of his destiny, willingly taking the road to the cross.

- Jesus's resurrection vindicates his claim to be the Messiah. With all authority bestowed on him by the Father, he now commissions his followers to make disciples of all nations, baptizing them in the name of the Father, the Son, and the Holy Spirit.

- Matthew's Christology has two main foci: Jesus as the Jewish Messiah fulfilling the promises given to Israel, and as Immanuel, the presence and wisdom of God, and now authoritative Lord of the church. The title Son of God is a particularly important one for Matthew, integrating these two portraits.

- Matthew's central theological theme is that salvation history finds its climax in the coming of Jesus the Messiah, inaugurator of the kingdom of heaven and the new age of salvation.

- By inaugurating the kingdom, Jesus does not "abolish" the law, but rather fulfills it, bringing it to its destined completion. New covenant believers are no longer under the old covenant, but under the new, inaugurated through Jesus's life, death, and resurrection. Standards of righteousness are even higher because the law is now written on the hearts of believers, who are guided and empowered by the Spirit of God.

- Matthew's theological themes suggest his primary narrative purpose is to confirm that Jesus is indeed the Messiah, and that the church, made up of Jews and Gentiles, are the people of God in the present age. He also writes to call God's people to experience and submit to the abiding presence and authority of Jesus in the church.

Reflection Questions

1. What are the key themes of the five major discourses in Matthew's Gospel?

2. Who are the main characters in Matthew's genealogy and why?

3. What apparent contradiction surrounds Jesus's teaching about the law? How would you resolve this difficulty?

Essay Question

1. What structural features are evident in Matthew's Gospel? What is a fulfillment formula? Explain the two main structural signals that have been identified with Matthew's "outline."

Quiz

1. (T/F) Matthew seldom uses language that would imply Jesus's deity.

2. (T/F) When Jesus commissions and sends out the Twelve in Matthew 10, he tells them to go only to "the lost sheep of Israel," not yet to the Gentiles.

3. (T/F) The religious leaders play a more positive role in Matthew's Gospel than in Mark's.

4. (T/F) According to the text, the community to which Matthew was writing was mostly Gentile, with a few Jews present.

5. (T/F) In Matthew, the disciples are portrayed in a somewhat more positive light than in Mark.

6. In quotations from the Old Testament, Matthew's Gospel follows:
   a) The Hebrew text of the Old Testament
   b) The Septuagint, the Greek version of the Hebrew Scriptures
   c) The Aramaic Targums, paraphrases of the Hebrew Scriptures
   d) At some places the Hebrew text; at others the Septuagint

7. The voice from heaven at Jesus's baptism alludes to both Psalm 2:7 ("This is my beloved son . . .") and Isaiah 42:1 (". . . with him I am well pleased"). The former confirms that Jesus is the Messiah and Son of God, the latter confirms he is _____.
   a) The prophet like Moses
   b) The Son of Man
   c) The Servant of the Lord
   d) The son of David

8. According to the text, there are two main portraits that control Matthew's Christology. The first is Jesus as the Messiah, the fulfillment of God's promises; the second is:

a) Jesus as the Incarnate Word made flesh
b) Jesus as Immanuel, the presence and wisdom of God
c) Jesus as the Son of Man, coming in the clouds of heaven
d) Jesus as the Good Shepherd, who cares for the flock of God

9. According to the text, which of the following statements best represents Matthew's perspective on the Law?

a) Jesus affirms that believers must continue to keep the Old Testament Law
b) Jesus abolishes the Old Testament Law and replaces it with the New Covenant Law of Grace
c) Jesus fulfills or completes the Old Testament Law, establishing a New Covenant where the Law is written on believer's hearts, rather than on stone
d) None of the above

10. According to the text, Matthew's *primary* narrative purpose is to confirm:

a) The humanity and deity of Jesus Christ
b) That Jesus is the Jewish Messiah who fulfills God's promises
c) Salvation by faith alone, apart from the works of the law
d) The atoning and sacrificial significance of Christ's death on the cross

CHAPTER 9

Luke

The Gospel of the Savior of the World

You Should Know

- Luke and Acts form a theological and narrative unity (Luke-Acts), sharing a common purpose and common theological themes.

- The central theme of Luke-Acts is *the arrival of God's end-time salvation*. As predicted in the prophets, through Jesus the Messiah God has acted to save his people Israel, and this salvation is now going forth to the whole world.

- Important sub-themes include (a) the Spirit as a sign of God's end time salvation, (b) the sovereign purpose of God, (c) salvation for outsiders, (d) joy and praise in response to God's salvation, (e) Jerusalem and the temple as settings of rejection and salvation, (f) Jesus's prayer life and intimacy with the Father.

- Luke's birth narrative (Luke 1–2) presents Jesus as the promised Messiah from the line of David, anxiously awaited by the righteous remnant of Israel. Key features include the parallels between the births of John and Jesus, and the hymns or praise songs which carry the story forward.

- Jesus's Nazareth sermon (4:14–30) sets the stage for the rest of the Gospel by demonstrating God's concern for Gentiles and foreshadowing Israel's rejection of her Messiah.

- Jesus's Galilean ministry in Luke reveals the reception of the gospel by outsiders, outcasts, and the lowly, while the proud and self-righteous miss out.

- The question of Jesus's identity, posed throughout the Galilean ministry, is answered in Peter's confession, "You are the God's Messiah" (9:18–27). As in Matthew and Mark, this episode marks a key turning point as Jesus begins teaching about his suffering fate in Jerusalem.

- The journey to Jerusalem (travel narrative) climaxes with the story of Zacchaeus and the parable of the minas, which reaffirm God's love for the lost (Luke 19:10) and the need for faithful stewardship after his departure.

- Jesus's trial and crucifixion are marked by the recurrent Christological theme of Jesus's innocence. He is the righteous and innocent Servant of the Lord (Isaiah 53).

- The account of the Emmaus disciples is Luke's most important contribution to the resurrection narratives. Its theme is the fulfillment of Scripture through the death of the Messiah.

Reflection Questions

1. What do we mean by the "unity" of Luke-Acts? How does Luke's literary style compare to the other Gospels?

2. What is the main emphasis of Luke's genealogy? How does it compare to Matthew's?

3. What are the main features of Jesus's Galilean ministry?

Essay Question

1. Identify some of the important sub-themes and state how they relate to the central theme of Luke-Acts.

Quiz

1. (T/F) Luke identifies Jesus as a great prophet.

2. (T/F) Women play a less prominent role in Luke's Gospel than in the other three Gospels.

3. (T/F) According to the text, the *primary* character trait of the religious leaders in Luke is that they are unredeemable and intractably lost.

4. (T/F) Only Luke relates that at the transfiguration, Jesus, Moses, and Elijah were discussing Jesus's coming "departure" or exodus in Jerusalem.

5. (T/F) The journey to Jerusalem (also known as the "gospel to the outcasts") climaxes with the transfiguration.

6. The evidence from the New Testament indicates that Luke was:
   a) A companion of the apostle Paul
   b) A Gentile
   c) A physician
   d) All of the above

7. The important place given to the Holy Spirit in Luke-Acts is primarily to demonstrate:
   a) That the Holy Spirit will bring conviction of sin to the world
   b) That the coming of the Holy Spirit heralds the dawn of the new age of salvation
   c) That the Holy Spirit will bring to remembrance all that Jesus taught the disciples
   d) All of the above

8. Luke's most significant contribution to the Gospel resurrection narratives is the account of:
   a) Peter's restoration by the Sea of Galilee
   b) Jesus's appearance to Mary Magdalene
   c) Jesus's appearance to the Emmaus disciples
   d) Jesus's appearance to Thomas

9. According to the text, the central Christological theme of Jesus's passion narrative in Luke is:
   a) Jesus's innocence as the righteous servant of the Lord
   b) The failure of the disciples contrasted with Jesus's faithfulness
   c) Jesus's death as a sacrificial atonement for sins
   d) Jesus as the victorious Son of God

10. The important episode that Luke brings forward from its position in Mark 6 in order to highlight it at the beginning of Jesus's ministry is:

    a) The baptism of Jesus
    b) The temptation of Jesus
    c) The Nazareth sermon
    d) The transfiguration

CHAPTER 10

John

The Gospel of the Son Who Reveals the Father

You Should Know

- John's Gospel is unique among the Gospels, with a distinct literary style and much unique content.

- John often refers to Jesus's opponents as *Ioudaioi* ("Jews" or "Jewish leaders") suggesting that he is writing to a community that has broken away from the larger Jewish community.

- The Gospel has four sections: (a) Prologue, (b) Book of Signs (seven miracles together with teaching and dialogue), (c) Book of Glory (the Last Supper and passion narratives), (d) Epilogue.

- The Gospel is full of metaphors and symbols, with much verbal and situational irony.

- The feeding of the five thousand (ch. 6) is the only miracle to appear in all four Gospels. Jesus is the bread of life who provides true spiritual manna, recalling the Passover festival.

- In his teaching at the Feast of Tabernacles (chs. 7–8), Jesus draws on festival symbols to identify himself as living water and the light of the world. He also identifies himself as the "I am"—the divine name of God from Exodus 3:14.

- As in the Synoptics, Jesus's triumphal entry serves as a public announcement of his messiahship (Zech. 9:9).

- The Book of Glory (chs. 13–20) begins with the Last Supper narrative. Jesus washes the disciples' feet, teaches on servanthood and love, and gives his farewell discourse (chs. 14–16). He promises to send the Spirit as teacher, comforter, and guide during his absence. The disciples are called to "abide" in him.

- The main theme of the trial and crucifixion in John is that Jesus is in control of his destiny and is acting according to God's plan (chs. 18–19).

- John's resurrection narrative is unique in Jesus's appearance to Mary Magdalene alone, and in appearances to the disciples first without and then with Thomas present. Thomas's confession "My Lord and my God!" frames (an *inclusio*) the entire Gospel between two acclamations of Jesus's deity (1:1; 20:28).

- John's Gospel presents the most exalted Christology in the New Testament. Jesus is the pre-existent Logos, the Son of God who perfectly reveals the Father and brings people into relationship with him.

- John provides a dualistic perspective where Jesus represents light, truth, and life, and stands against Satan and the evil world system, representing darkness, deceit, and death.

- John's primary narrative purpose is to call people to faith in Jesus the Christ and Son of God so that they might have eternal life in his name (20:30, 31).

- The identification of the Beloved Disciple with the apostle John has been the historical position of the church. Though not without some problems, it fits well with both internal and external evidence.

- John's Gospel was likely written in the late first century and was likely composed by the apostle John while he was ministering in Ephesus.

Reflection Questions

1. What is the main theme of John's trial and crucifixion narrative?

2. Summarize the Christology of John's Gospel.

3. How is the theme of salvation presented in John's Gospel and how is this different than the Synoptics?

Essay Question

1. How is John unique among the Gospels? What kinds of Synoptic material does John *not* include in his Gospel? Identify the basic four-fold structure of John.

Quiz

1. (T/F) While John presents Jesus as equal with God the Father, he also strongly emphasizes Jesus's functional subordination to the Father.

2. (T/F) The Greek term *Ioudaioi* ("the Jews") is common in the Synoptics, but very rare in John.

3. (T/F) The text concludes that the Beloved Disciple is most likely John the apostle.

4. (T/F) In contrast to Luke-Acts, John emphasizes the role of the Holy Spirit as the fulfillment of prophecy.

5. (T/F) Jesus's interview with Nicodemus parallels and is set in contrast to his interview with the Samaritan woman.

6. The primary purpose of the signs in John is to:
    a) Demonstrate the power of the kingdom of God
    b) Reveal Jesus's glory and provoke faith in him
    c) Confirm the authenticity of Jesus's exorcisms and healings
    d) All of the above

7. According to the text, what background does John draw from when he uses the term *Logos* ("Word") in John 1?
    a) The Jewish concept of personified Wisdom
    b) The Old Testament concept of the dynamic force of God's will: He speaks and it is done

c) The Greek philosophical idea of divine reason
d) All of the above

8. In John 5, Jesus justifies his healing on the Sabbath by pointing out that:

a) People have authority over the Sabbath
b) He is Lord of the Sabbath
c) God works on the Sabbath and so Jesus does also
d) Christians will from now on worship on Sunday, not Saturday

9. According to the text, the central theme of John's Gospel is:

a) Salvation by grace through faith
b) The dawn of end time salvation and coming of the kingdom of God
c) The revelation of the Father through the Son
d) The fulfillment of the Old Testament through Jesus the Messiah

10. In John's Gospel, in contrast to the Synoptics, eternal life is especially emphasized as:

a) A future inheritance
b) A present possession
c) A past reality
d) A special gift to come

CHAPTER 11

Searching for the Real Jesus

You Should Know

- Controlled by Enlightenment-era rationalism, the nineteenth century "Quest for the Historical Jesus" (the First Quest) sought to establish Jesus as a non-supernatural teacher of love and humanistic philosophy.

- Albert Schweitzer's classic book *The Quest for the Historical Jesus* undermined the First Quest by showing that authors created a Jesus in their own image.

- Building on the work of Schweitzer, Wrede, Weiss, Kähler, and others, Rudolf Bultmann's radical skepticism led to a period of "No Quest," when many scholars considered the historical Jesus both unattainable and irrelevant.

- The New (Second) Quest was launched by E. Käsemann and other students of Bultmann. Yet by adopting much of their teacher's skepticism, the New Quest produced only a minimalist portrait of Jesus.

- The Third Quest is a name given to the spate of recent Jesus scholarship which utilizes a variety of new methodologies.

- Sometimes viewed as part of the Third Quest, sometimes distinct, the Jesus Seminar is a group of scholars who have met to vote on the sayings and deeds of Jesus. The Seminar rejects as unhistorical most of the sayings and stories in the Gospels.

- Conclusions about Jesus are determined by many factors: the sources examined, the criteria utilized, the method employed, the historical context presumed, and the worldview of the investigator.

- The "criteria of authenticity" are used by scholars to test the historicity of the words and deeds of Jesus. The most basic is the criterion of dissimilarity, which claims sayings of Jesus are authentic if they are unique from Judaism and early Christianity.

- While potentially effective tools, the criteria are open to subjectivity and abuse. Researchers often find only the Jesus they are looking for.

- Five main portraits of Jesus are developed by contemporary Jesus scholars: cynic-sage, spirit person, social revolutionary, eschatological prophet, and Messiah.

Reflection Questions

1. Summarize the significance of E. Troeltsch, D. F. Strauss, J. Weiss, W. Wrede, M. Kähler, and the history-of-religions school for historical Jesus studies. Who is R. Bultmann, and what was his perspective?

2. What were the First Quest, New (Second) Quest, and Third Quest, and what were their characteristics?

3. What is the Jesus Seminar? What were its goals? What were its conclusions?

Essay Question

1. Describe in summary the five main portraits of Jesus: cynic-like philosopher, spirit-endowed holy man, social revolutionary, eschatological prophet, and Messiah.

Quiz

1. (T/F) The premise of the history of religions school was that all religions develop from simple to complex.

2. (T/F) E. Käsemann's *Life of Christ Critically Examined* was one of the first attempts to explain the supernatural elements in the Gospels with the concept of "myth."

3. (T/F) William Wrede's view on the "messianic secret" in Mark portrayed the Gospel writers as theologians rather than historians.

4. (T/F) Richard Horsely claims Jesus was a social revolutionary attempting to reform society with a radical reorganization of village life.

5. (T/F) Bultmann did not draw a strict distinction between the Jesus of history and the Christ of faith.

6. The most radical attacks on the historical Jesus in recent years (1980–90s) have come from:

    a) The participants of the "First Quest" for the historical Jesus
    b) The participants of the "New Quest" for the historical Jesus
    c) The participants of the "Third Quest" for the historical Jesus
    d) The participants of the Jesus Seminar

7. This criterion draws on the conclusions of source criticism related to Mark, Q, and other early sources for the Jesus tradition.

    a) The criterion of multiple attestation
    b) The criterion of coherence
    c) The criterion of dissimilarity
    d) The criterion of Semitic flavor

8. The most basic of the so-called criteria of authenticity—it claims that a saying of Jesus is authentic if it appears neither in the teaching of Judaism nor in the teaching of first-century Christianity.

    a) The criterion of coherence
    b) The criterion of multiple attestation
    c) The criterion of dissimilarity
    d) The criterion of Semitic flavor

9. This view is espoused by E. P. Sanders, John P. Meier, and others. It claims Jesus was expecting the imminent arrival of God's kingdom.

    a) Social revolutionary
    b) Jewish mystic or spirit person
    c) Cynic-like philosopher
    d) Eschatological prophet

10. This view is held by John Dominic Crossan and most of the Jesus Seminar. It views Jesus as a wandering counter-cultural peasant preacher.

   a) Social revolutionary
   b) Jewish mystic or spirit person
   c) Cynic-like philosopher
   d) Eschatological prophet

CHAPTER 12

The Historical Reliability of the Gospels

You Should Know

- While no one reads the Gospels without presuppositions, this does not mean all truth is relative. Historical events can be judged by carefully weighing the evidence.

- The fact that the Gospel writers have strong faith commitments does not negate their historical reliability.

- All historians have a worldview and a belief system which motivates their writing.

- Luke's skill as a historian has been demonstrated especially in Acts, where he is a meticulous researcher with reference to names, places, and titles. Luke also demonstrates a keen sense of the *Zeitgeist*, or "spirit of the times," in which he writes.

- Evidence for the general reliability of the gospel tradition includes (a) the value given to eyewitness testimony, (b) the pattern of careful oral transmission in Palestinian Judaism, (c) the church's willingness to preserve difficult sayings, (d) the distinction made between the words of Jesus and of Christian prophets, (e) the absence of created sayings on issues of later concern to the church, and (f) the high ethical standards of the disciples.

- Apparent contradictions in the Gospels often disappear when it is recognized that the Evangelists were not producing verbatim accounts, but had the freedom to paraphrase, interpret, abbreviate, and reorder events and sayings to fit their theological purpose. They were not just reporters, but inspired interpreters of the Jesus event.

- Though the reliability of John's Gospel has been questioned even more than the Synoptics, recent research has produced greater respect for its historicity.

- Jesus's unique style of speaking in John is not as different from the Synoptics as is sometimes supposed, and may be explained by a combination of John's paraphrase of Jesus's teaching and his Spirit-inspired interpretation of Jesus's words.

- It is ultimately a false dichotomy to contrast the historical and theological features of the Gospels. Good history can also be good theology.

Reflection Questions

1. Explain why it isn't possible to write or read history without presuppositions and a worldview.

2. Do the faith commitments of the Gospel writers negate their claim to writing accurate history? Why or why not?

3. What is some of the evidence that Luke was an accurate historian? What is the evidence for the historical reliability of John?

Essay Question

1. What is the evidence for a generally reliable gospel tradition? How might we explain some of the apparent contradictions among the Gospels?

Quiz

1. (T/F) Although in John's Gospel Jesus speaks frequently of the relationship between the Father and the Son, this manner of speaking never occurs in the Synoptic Gospels.

2. (T/F) New Testament scholars have long recognized that in most cases we have the exact words of Jesus.

3. (T/F) All four Gospel writers follow chronological order as they report events.

4. (T/F) Most of the alleged contradictions between John and the Synoptics are quite easily explained by recognizing that John interpreted his material in such a way as to emphasize particular themes.

5. (T/F) John is the only Gospel writer who presents a high Christology.

6. Which of the following is NOT evidence cited in the text for a reliable gospel tradition?
   a) The many stories shared in common by Matthew, Mark, and Luke
   b) The church's willingness to preserve difficult sayings of Jesus
   c) The absence of gospel discussion of key issues raised in the later church
   d) The testimony of eyewitnesses

7. The phrase *ipsissima verba*, which we generally do not have in the Gospels, means:
   a) The authentic voice of Jesus
   b) The exact words that Jesus spoke
   c) Fictional expansions on Jesus's words
   d) The words given to the apostles

8. Which Gospel writer most often abbreviates accounts which are told in more detail in other Gospels?
   a) Matthew
   b) Mark
   c) Luke
   d) John

9. In Matthew's Gospel, Jesus's temptation account climaxes:
   a) In the temple
   b) On a high mountain

    c) On the Mount of Transfiguration
    d) In Nazareth

10. Doublets are:

    a) A pattern of Hebrew poetry similar to synonymous parallelism
    b) Two gospel episodes that some scholars claim arose from the same story
    c) A story which appears in the "double tradition" (Matthew and Luke = "Q")
    d) A dualistic worldview contrasting things like light and darkness

CHAPTER 13

The Contours and Chronology of Jesus's Ministry

You Should Know

- Core features of Jesus's ministry (agreed upon by almost everyone) include: the prophetic ministry of John the Baptist, the baptism of Jesus by John, Jesus's preaching about the kingdom of God and healing ministry in Galilee, growing opposition by Jewish religious authorities, Jerusalem ministry during which there was an incident in the temple, arrest by Jewish and/or Roman authorities, trial of some sort by Jewish and/or Roman authorities, execution by the Romans ordered by Pontius Pilate, followed by reports of his resurrection by his disciples.

- Jesus was born sometime between 7–4 BC during the reign of Herod the Great.

- Prior to Jesus, "prophets" and "messiahs" had arisen with bold claims of deliverance and were rejected by the religious authorities.

- Jesus's public ministry probably occurred either from AD 27–30 or AD 30–33. Both dates have supportive evidence, though the earlier one is perhaps more likely.

- Jesus was likely crucified on Friday, Nisan 15 (Passover), in either AD 30 or 33.

- John the Baptist would have reminded people of the prophets in the Old Testament.

- Jesus's central message concerned the coming of God's kingdom.

- John's baptism in the Jordan was a symbol of God's cleansing of the people's hearts.

- Jesus generally avoided conflict with the political authorities.

- Jesus's reputation as a rabbi made his behavior scandalous among the religious leaders.

Reflection Questions

1. Between what years was Jesus born? Who was reigning in Israel at the time?

2. About how old was Jesus when his public ministry began? How do we know this?

3. What are the most likely dates for Jesus's public ministry and for his crucifixion? During what Jewish festival was Jesus crucified?

Essay Question

1. Identify the key features of Jesus's ministry which are agreed upon by almost everyone.

Quiz

1. (T/F) The average Palestinian did not view Jesus as sent from God.

2. (T/F) The Pharisees were admired for their piety and spiritual devotion.

3. (T/F) Zealots were known for loving their enemies.

4. (T/F) Jesus was called Rabbi because he had formal training.

5. (T/F) The average Palestinian would have clearly understood Jesus's words.

6. Which of the following is NOT one of the almost undisputed facts about Jesus's life (held by scholars of all theological stripes):

   a) His baptism by John the Baptist
   b) His reputation as a healer and exorcist
   c) His claim to be the Messiah and Son of God
   d) His arrest and crucifixion in Jerusalem

7. Jesus was born around:

   a) AD 30
   b) 7–4 BC
   c) 1 BC
   d) 0

8. Which Gospel tells us Jesus was "about thirty years old" when his ministry began?

   a) Matthew
   b) Mark
   c) Luke
   d) John

9. Which Gospel provides us with the most information concerning the length of Jesus's ministry?

   a) Matthew
   b) Mark
   c) Luke
   d) John

10. The two most likely dates for the year of Jesus's crucifixion are either AD 30 or:

   a) 4 BC
   b) AD 27
   c) AD 33
   d) AD 70

CHAPTER 14

Jesus's Birth and Childhood

You Should Know

- Though the birth narratives serve as theological introductions to the Gospels of Matthew and Luke, they also contain reliable traditions concerning the birth and childhood of Jesus.

- The differences between the two genealogies can be plausibly explained in various ways. They may represent, respectively, the genealogies of Joseph and Mary, a royal genealogy versus physical genealogy, or Joseph's natural genealogy versus a legal one (through adoption or levirate marriage).

- There is little evidence to suggest that Jesus's virginal conception was a myth created by the church to fulfill prophecy. Matthew and Luke independently attest to it, and Luke does not explicitly link it to Isaiah 7:14. The event confirms that Jesus's conception was a supernatural act of God, bringing together the human and divine in one person.

- While some scholars claim Jesus was born in Nazareth, Matthew and Luke independently attest to Jesus's Bethlehem birth. Since Luke does not mention Micah 5:2, it is unlikely that the tradition was created around this prophecy.

- The "inn" from which Jesus's parents were turned away was probably not an ancient hotel, but the sleeping quarters of a private residence. Because of crowded conditions, Jesus was born in a humble place reserved for animals.

- The magi, probably court astrologers from Persia or Arabia, arrived as much as two years after Jesus's birth, while his family was living in a house in Bethlehem.

- Herod's attempt to kill the infants of Bethlehem fits well with his character as a cruel and despotic ruler. Considering Herod's many atrocities, it is not surprising that this minor event is not recorded by Josephus or other historians.

- Jesus likely had an ordinary childhood growing up in a conservative Jewish home. He had four brothers and some sisters, and would have learned carpentry from his father. Luke's account of his childhood visit to Jerusalem confirms Jesus's growing awareness of a unique father-son relationship with God.

Reflection Questions

1. What are the main differences between the genealogies of Matthew and Luke and what are some possible solutions to the problem of two different genealogies?

2. What are some of the problems and possible solutions concerning the census associated with Jesus's birth?

3. Identify some common misconceptions related to the birth of Jesus, such as the nature of the "inn," the number of wise men, and the time of their arrival.

Essay Question

1. What is the evidence that Matthew and Luke are using historical traditions in their birth narratives, rather than merely creating stories to fit their theological agendas?

Quiz

1. (T/F) Both Matthew and Luke affirm Jesus's Davidic ancestry.

2. (T/F) The census that brought Joseph and Mary to Bethlehem is clearly attested in secular Roman sources.

3. (T/F) Joseph's occupation, traditionally translated "carpenter," referred to a craftsman who worked in wood, stone, or metal.

4. (T/F) Matthew's birth narrative starts with Jesus and works back to Abraham.

5. (T/F) The birth narrative of Jesus is very different from those of pagan myths.

6. Matthew records Jesus's "royal" genealogy through David's son:
   - a) Solomon
   - b) Nathan
   - c) Jonathan
   - d) Goliath

7. The traditional translation that Mary and Joseph could find no room at the "inn" probably meant either a "caravan shelter" or a:
   - a) Cave where travelers would sleep
   - b) Guest room in a private home
   - c) Town square
   - d) Roadside inn or hotel

8. The magi, or "wise men," who appear in Matthew's account were likely:
   - a) Kings
   - b) Philosophers
   - c) Bedouin
   - d) Astrologers

9. The Gospels report that Jesus had ___ brothers and several sisters.
   - a) 2
   - b) 3
   - c) 4
   - d) 5

10. Jesus grew up near the thriving Hellenistic-Jewish city called:

a) Caesarea
b) Sepphoris
c) Tyre
d) Sychar

CHAPTER 15

The Beginning of Jesus's Ministry

You Should Know

- John the Baptist is presented in all four Gospels as the precursor for Jesus, the prophetic herald of messianic salvation.

- John the Baptist's dress is reminiscent of the prophet Elijah. His ministry was across the Jordan from Samaria.

- John's water baptism has antecedents in Jewish ceremonial cleansings and proselyte baptism, but is best viewed as a unique application symbolizing a person's repentance and preparation for the kingdom of God.

- John was imprisoned and eventually executed by Herod Antipas after criticizing Herod for his divorce and remarriage to Herodias, his brother Philip's wife.

- Jesus's baptism by John is one of the most undisputed events in his life. It marks Jesus's "anointing" as Messiah and empowering for ministry. The voice from heaven, echoing Psalm 2:7, Isaiah 42:1, and Genesis 22:2, implicitly identifies Jesus as the Messiah who will offer himself as a sacrifice for sins.

- Jesus's temptation is analogous to both Adam and Eve in the Garden, and also the testing of Israel in the wilderness.

- Only the Gospel of Luke provides information concerning the early life of John the Baptist.

- Some speculate that John the Baptist may have had contact with the monastic community at Qumran.

Reflection Questions

1. What is the possible background to John's "baptism of repentance"? Why might Jesus have submitted to John's baptism?

2. What might be the significance of the dove? Of the Old Testament allusions in the voice from heaven?

3. What is the main theme of the temptation account?

Essay Question

1. What role does John the Baptist play in the gospel tradition? What Old Testament verses are used to describe him? How did Jesus describe him?

Quiz

1. (T/F) John the Baptist never doubted that Jesus was the Messiah.

2. (T/F) According to the text, Jesus's temptation may have been a visionary experience.

3. (T/F) It is very clear that first-century Judaism practiced proselyte baptism.

4. (T/F) John the Baptist stated that the one coming after him would baptize only with the Holy Spirit.

5. (T/F) Jesus was the only one who witnessed the Spirit's descent at his baptism.

6. (T/F) Josephus believed that Herod was most afraid that John the Baptist would provoke an uprising.

7. Which of the following is (apart from the crucifixion) the most undisputed historical event of Jesus's life?

   a) Jesus was born in Bethlehem
   b) Jesus was baptized by John

c) Jesus was tempted by Satan in the wilderness
d) Jesus fed the multitudes with a few loaves and fishes

8. A Jewish immersion pool used for ceremonial cleansing was called a:

a) *Mikveh*
b) *Phylactery*
c) *Shofar*
d) *Targum*

9. John the Baptist was executed by:

a) Pontius Pilate
b) Herod the Great
c) Herod Antipas
d) Caiaphas

10. It is a common pattern in the Old Testament and in Judaism for commissioning by God to be followed by:

a) Blessing
b) Testing
c) Time for contemplation
d) Honor

CHAPTER 16

The Message of Jesus

You Should Know

- Jesus's central message concerned the coming of the kingdom of God. The kingdom is both a present reality and a future hope. God's end time salvation has been inaugurated in the present through Jesus's words and deeds and will be consummated in the future when the Son of Man returns in glory. It is both "already" and "not yet."

- Concerning the law of Moses, Jesus (a) emphasizes the true meaning and spirit of the law, a reflection of God's righteous character, and (b) identifies himself as the fulfillment of the law, establishing a *new* covenant through his righteous life and death on the cross.

- Jesus's teaching about the law looks past the law given at Mount Sinai to the very character of God who gave the law. The whole law can be summed up in the love commandment because this reflects the fundamental nature of God, who is absolute love.

- Jesus's teaching on poverty and wealth must be seen as both literal and spiritual. Entering the kingdom of God requires the repudiation of self-sufficiency of every kind and humble dependence on God.

- Jesus's parables used vivid and memorable scenes from everyday life to teach profound spiritual truth. While all the features of the parables must not be allegorized, many parables do contain allegorical elements.

- To understand the parables it is important (a) to interpret them first and foremost in the context of Jesus's ministry, (b) to relate them to his preaching of the kingdom of God, (c) to recognize their cultural and literary background in the OT and Judaism, (d) to seek the primary point of the parable, (e) to exercise caution concerning allegorical elements, and (f) to determine the narrative function of the parable in the Gospel in which it appears.

- Hyperbole: an exaggeration used for emphasis
- Year of Jubilee: Old Testament language Jesus referred to as the "year of the Lord's favor"

Reflection Questions

1. Did Jesus affirm the validity of the OT law or did he overrule it? What is the solution to this apparent paradox?

2. How can we reconcile Jesus's teaching on God's free grace offered to sinners, and the high cost of discipleship?

3. Identify key principles for interpreting the parables.

Essay Question

1. What was Jesus's central message? What is the OT and Jewish background to the kingdom of God? What did Jesus mean by the "kingdom of God"? How do the present and future dimensions of the kingdom relate to one another?

Quiz

1. (T/F) In the Jewish literature of Jesus's time, the kingdom of God referred only to God's sovereign reign over the universe, not a future kingdom that God would establish on earth.

2. (T/F) When Jesus speaks of blessings for the "poor," he is referring only to spiritual poverty, not physical poverty.

3. (T/F) Jesus claimed that the kingdom of God would begin arriving after his death.

4. (T/F) Jesus never altered or even seemed to ignore aspects of the law.

5. (T/F) The "tradition of the elders" was the oral law later transcribed in the rabbinic writings.

6. Adolf Jülicher claimed that Jesus's parables:

    a) Were not allegories, but similitudes, or extended similes
    b) Must be interpreted allegorically
    c) Had multiple meanings
    d) Were mostly inauthentic

7. According to the text, the best description of Jesus's relationship to the law is that:

    a) Jesus abolished the Mosaic law
    b) Jesus abolished the ceremonial aspects of the law, but kept the moral aspects
    c) Jesus fulfilled the whole law, transforming it for all time
    d) Jesus reaffirmed the whole law and encouraged believers to keep it

8. Jesus taught that God's kingdom was:

    a) A present reality
    b) A future inheritance
    c) Both of the above
    d) Neither of the above

9. "Jesus said to them, 'I have shown you many good works from the Father. For which of these do you stone me?'" (John 10:32) uses the literary device called:

    a) Irony
    b) Hyperbole
    c) Simile
    d) Pun

10. "For whoever wants to save their life will lose it, but whoever loses their life for me will save it" (Luke 9:24) uses the literary device called:

a) Simile
b) Paradox
c) Pun
d) Metaphor

CHAPTER 17

The Miracles of Jesus

You Should Know

- The question of miracles must be examined first philosophically, concerning their logical possibility, and then historically, concerning their actual occurrence.

- Contrary to the claims of David Hume, no valid philosophical argument mitigates against the possibility of supernatural intervention in the so-called laws of nature.

- Historically, miracles should be accepted if there is enough historical evidence to confirm it with a high degree of probability.

- There is near universal agreement that Jesus was viewed by his contemporaries as a healer and exorcist.

- Parallels between Jesus's miracles and those of first-century magicians, Hellenistic "divine-men," or charismatic holy men are unconvincing, making it unlikely that the church created the gospel miracle tradition in imitation of these.

- Jesus's miracles reveal the power and presence of the kingdom in his actions. The healings and exorcisms symbolize the reversal of the curse and the defeat of sin and Satan. The resuscitations reveal the power of the final resurrection with the coming of the kingdom.

- The so-called nature miracles function as enacted parables, revealing the in-breaking power of the kingdom and the dawn of the new age of salvation.

- Deism: the philosophical system claiming God created the world, but then left it to run wholly by natural laws

- Descartes: the most significant philosophical opposition to the miraculous came from the eighteenth-century philosopher

- Materialism: the philosophical assumption that the world is a closed system of cause and effect without divine intervention

Reflection Questions

1. Why do most historians accept that Jesus had a reputation as a healer and exorcist? What is the evidence for this?

2. To what ancient parallels have Jesus's miracles been compared? What similarities and differences were there between Jesus and so-called divine men? What similarities and differences between Jesus and charismatic holy men?

3. According to Jesus's own teaching, what was the significance of his exorcisms? His healings? The revivations? The nature miracles?

Essay Question

1. In what ways is the question of miracles both a philosophical one and a historical one? How would you answer David Hume's objections to miracles?

Quiz

1. (T/F) While the study of miracles is outside the realm of strict scientific investigation — which involves repeatability and observation — it is not outside the realm of historical research, which depends on written and oral reports.

2. (T/F) Almost all New Testament scholars—whether liberal or conservative—accept that Jesus was widely acclaimed as an exorcist and healer.

3. (T/F) Jesus considered his exorcisms a spiritual assault on the dominion of Satan.

4. (T/F) Jewish sources outside of the New Testament also refer to Jesus's miracles.

5. (T/F) Jesus is the only person historians know of who performed healings and exorcisms.

6. Jesus's miracles show some similarities to the first-century Hellenistic wonder-worker (or divine man) from Tyana known as:
    a) Simon Magus
    b) Elymas bar Jesus
    c) Apollonius
    d) Cerinthus

7. The Jewish charismatic rabbi, whose prayers for rain were reportedly answered, was named:
    a) Simon Magus
    b) Honi
    c) Hillel
    d) Bar Kokhba

8. According to the text, the *primary* purpose for Jesus's healings and exorcisms in the Synoptic Gospels is:
    a) To reveal the deity of Christ
    b) To put the religious leaders to shame
    c) To bring glory to Jesus
    d) To reveal the presence and power of the kingdom of God

9. The accounts in the Gospels where Jesus raises people from the dead are best understood as:
    a) True resurrections from a Jewish perspective
    b) Resuscitations to mortal life
    c) Reception of glorified and immortal bodies
    d) None of the above

10. Which kinds of miracles are described in the text as "enacted parables"?
    a) Healings
    b) Raising the dead
    c) Nature miracles
    d) Exorcisms

CHAPTER 18

The Messianic Words and Actions of Jesus

You Should Know

- The actions, as well as the words, of Jesus can tell us a great deal about his self-understanding and his aims.

- Jesus's aims or intentions are seen in various ways:

  i. He appoints the Twelve, representing the remnant of Israel and the end-time people of God.

  ii. He associates with sinners and outcasts, offering them free forgiveness of sins in the new age of salvation.

  iii. He repeatedly hints that his message will go to the Gentiles, evidence that Isaiah's promise of light to the Gentiles is now being fulfilled (Isa. 42:6; 49:6).

  iv. Jesus's entry into Jerusalem on a donkey was an intentional enactment of Zechariah 9:9, indicating that Jesus is the peace-bringing king of Israel.

  v. Jesus's clearing the temple was likely a symbolic act of judgment, indicating that the age of temple worship was giving way to the new covenant age of salvation.

- Jesus's words and actions suggest he believed himself to be the Messiah, God's end-time agent of salvation.

- Son of Man, Jesus's favorite self-designation, emphasizes his true humanity and identifies him with the exalted messianic figure in Daniel 7:13–14, but avoids the political preconceptions associated with other titles like Messiah and son of David.

- The evidence is strong that Jesus considered himself the unique Son of God: the title is closely linked to Jesus's messiahship; the Aramaic term *Abba* ("Father") which Jesus used to address God is almost certainly authentic; several Synoptic passages where Jesus identifies himself as "the Son" have a good claim to authenticity (Mark 12:1–11; Mark 13:32/Matt. 24:36; Matthew 11:27/Luke 10:22).

- Passages like Mark 12:35–37 suggest that Jesus viewed himself as the exalted Lord, greater even than David.

- While Jesus did not explicitly identify himself as divine, his claims to speak and act with the authority of Yahweh come close and suggest that the church's later Christological confessions are a natural development of meditation on the significance of Jesus's person and work.

- Maranatha: an Aramaic word for "Our Lord Come!"

- Son of Man: Jesus's favorite title for himself

Reflection Questions

1. What claims did Jesus make which exhibit his extraordinary sense of authority?

2. What do the following features of Jesus's ministry indicate about his aims or purpose: his appointment of the Twelve; his association with sinners and outcasts; his attitude toward the Gentiles; his entrance into Jerusalem on a donkey; his clearing of the temple?

3. What does *maranatha* mean, and what is its significance for the early church?

Essay Question

1. Summarize the Jewish background of the following messianic titles: Messiah, Son of Man, Son of God, Lord. Summarize the evidence that Jesus identified himself with each of these titles. What did he mean by them?

Quiz

1. (T/F) Jesus's use of the address *Abba* in prayer to God suggests he claimed a unique relationship with the Father.

2. (T/F) The title "Lord" (*kyrios*) always refers to a divine being, or god.

3. (T/F) Although Jesus never explicitly identifies himself as "God" in the Synoptic Gospels, he speaks and acts with divine authority.

4. (T/F) Jesus was probably reticent about using the title Messiah because of its political and militaristic connotations.

5. (T/F) N. T. Wright argues that there was a widespread belief in Judaism at the beginning of the first century that Israel was still in exile, both spiritually and physically.

6. The Old Testament predictions concerning God's salvation and the Gentiles took two distinct streams in Judaism. With which did Jesus identify?

   a) The Gentiles will come to Israel as subject nations to pay tribute and to acknowledge God's sovereignty
   b) The Gentiles would be co-recipients of God's salvation, worshipping with Israel on Mount Zion
   c) Both of the above
   d) Neither of the above

7. In first-century Judaism, the title "son of God" could be used of:

   a) The historical kings of Israel from David's line
   b) The nation of Israel
   c) The coming Messiah
   d) All of the above

8. Jesus's description of the Son of Man coming on the clouds of heaven is drawn from the Old Testament passage:

   a) Isaiah 9:1–6
   b) Jeremiah 23:5–6
   c) Daniel 7:13–14
   d) Micah 5:2

9. Jesus's entrance into Jerusalem on a colt seems to be an intentional fulfillment of the messianic prophecy of:

   a) Isaiah 11:1–11
   b) Jeremiah 31
   c) Micah 5:2
   d) Zechariah 9:9

10. The Greek word *amēn* comes from a Hebrew word meaning:

   a) The end or conclusion
   b) Confirmed or verified
   c) Praise the Lord
   d) The Lord has spoken

CHAPTER 19

The Death of Jesus

You Should Know

- The evidence suggests that both Roman and Jewish authorities were active participants in the arrest and trial of Jesus. The crucifixion was ordered by Pilate and carried out by Roman soldiers.

- Pilate probably acted against Jesus to placate the temple leadership, to prevent a popular revolt, and to serve as a grim warning against other troublemakers.

- The Jewish authorities probably acted against Jesus because he threatened their influence among the people and because he directly challenged their legitimacy as guardians of Torah and temple.

- During the Passion week, Jesus found the money changers in the Court of the Gentiles.

- The significance Jesus gave to his coming death can be discerned through his eucharistic words at the Last Supper and the ransom saying of Mark 10:45, both of which have strong claims to authenticity. Together these indicate that Jesus saw his death as a sacrificial death for the sins of his people, bringing spiritual freedom through a new exodus and establishing a new covenant relationship with God.

- At his last supper, Jesus inaugurated a new Passover celebration for the new age of salvation—the kingdom of God.

- Jesus carried his cross to the place of the skull where he was crucified.

- The opposition Jesus faced during his Galilean ministry was primarily from the Pharisees and the scribes.

- The Pharisees considered themselves the rightful guardians of Israel's traditions.

Reflection Questions

1. What role did the Roman authorities and the Jewish religious leaders likely play in the arrest, trial, and crucifixion of Jesus?

2. Why did Pilate act against Jesus?

3. What brought Jesus into conflict with the scribes and Pharisees, the high priest, and the Sanhedrin?

Essay Question

1. What is the evidence that Jesus foresaw and predicted his own death? What significance did Jesus give to his death? What evidence is there for the historicity of Jesus's eucharistic words and of the ransom saying of Mark 10:45?

Quiz

1. (T/F) Most contemporary scholars today acknowledged that both the Romans and the Jewish authorities must have played some role in Jesus's death.

2. (T/F) The evidence confirms that Jesus was executed by the Romans under the charge of sedition—rebellion against the government.

3. (T/F) Historical evidence confirms that in Jesus's day, the charge of blasphemy could be made against someone only for pronouncing the divine name, not for idolatry, arrogant disrespect for God, or insulting God's chosen leaders.

4. (T/F) Jesus repeatedly identified himself with the persecuted and suffering prophets of the Old Testament.

5. (T/F) When Jesus "cleansed" the temple, he would have raised the greatest opposition from the scribes and Pharisees.

6. (T/F) Crucifixion was a Jewish method of execution.

7. The closest parallel to Jesus's "ransom saying" of Mark 10:45 is:
   a) The portrait of righteous sufferers in the psalms
   b) The martyrdom tradition of the Maccabees and other Jewish heroes
   c) The suffering servant passage of Isaiah 53
   d) The glory to come at his Father's right hand in heaven

8. According to the text, Jesus was crucified for _____ reasons.
   a) Political
   b) Religious
   c) Both, since the two were inseparable in first-century Palestine
   d) Neither, since the Jews were the ones calling for his death

9. During Jesus's Galilean ministry, he faced opposition primarily from:
   a) The scribes and Pharisees
   b) The leading priests and Sadducees
   c) The Roman authorities
   d) The Essenes and Zealots

10. Which of these reasons was probably not a reason why Pilate had Jesus crucified?
   a) Doing it placated the Jewish leaders
   b) Doing it eliminated the possibility of people trying to make Jesus a king
   c) Doing it would please his Roman superiors
   d) Doing it would warn other would-be prophets and messiahs that Rome would stand for no dissent

CHAPTER 20

The Resurrection of Jesus

You Should Know

- Rationalistic explanations for the resurrection like the swoon theory, the wrong tomb theory, and the stolen body theory are generally rejected by scholars today.

- The most widely held rationalistic explanation is that the spiritual experiences of the disciples—especially through visions and dreams—that Jesus had been vindicated and exalted by God to his right hand, eventually developed into resurrection legends told and retold in the church.

- Five points of reliable historical evidence argue against this legendary-development view: (a) Jesus died by crucifixion in about AD 30; (b) he was buried in a tomb owned by Joseph of Arimathea; (c) the tomb was discovered empty on the third day after his death; (d) many reliable witnesses then saw Jesus alive; (e) this event transformed the lives of his closest followers.

- In its first-century Jewish context, the resurrection would have been understood not as a temporal event, but as the end time day of judgment, when God would raise the dead, punish the wicked, and reward the righteous.

- Jesus's resurrection must be understood within this context. It is not simply the restoration of physical life, but the beginning of the end time restoration of creation, the defeat of sin, Satan, and death.

- The Jewish claim that the disciples stole the body (Matt. 28:11–15) is indirect evidence for the resurrection, for it confirms that the tomb was empty.

- The Sadducees did not believe in the afterlife or the resurrection of the body.

- The women were told to tell the disciples to go to Galilee.

- Only Luke recounts Jesus's appearance to two disciples as they were traveling to Emmaus.

- The disciples received the Great Commission on a mountain in Galilee.

Reflection Questions

1. What was the significance of the resurrection of the dead in first-century Judaism?

2. In what sense is the resurrection of Jesus the beginning of the final resurrection?

3. How would Jesus likely have understood the resurrection in light of the teaching of Isaiah and other OT prophets?

Essay Question

1. Identify various rationalistic explanations for the resurrection. What is the most widely held rationalistic explanation today? What are the five pieces of highly reliable evidence which together support the historicity of the resurrection of Jesus?

Quiz

1. (T/F) Virtually no credible historians today deny that Jesus existed or that he was crucified in Judea under orders from Pontius Pilate around AD 30.

2. (T/F) In general, women were not viewed as reliable witnesses in first-century Palestinian culture.

3. (T/F) A theology of the resurrection is not well developed in the Old Testament.

4. (T/F) The arrival of God's kingdom meant that the last days had begun.

5. (T/F) Jesus's worldview was shaped by the restoration theology of Ezekiel.

6. Jesus's resurrection is viewed in the New Testament as:

   a) The renewal of mortal human existence
   b) A spiritual rather than bodily resurrection
   c) A unique event, completely different from the future resurrection of believers
   d) The beginning of the end-times resurrection of believers

7. The _____, like Jesus and Paul, believed in a future bodily resurrection when God would reward the righteous and judge the wicked.

   a) Pharisees
   b) Sadducees
   c) Stoics
   d) Cynics

8. This writer, who provides the earliest written testimony of the resurrection, claims that more than 500 people saw Jesus alive.

   a) Peter
   b) James
   c) John
   d) Paul

9. According to the Gospels, Jesus was buried in the tomb of _____.

   a) Nicodemus
   b) Caiaphas
   c) Joseph of Arimathea
   d) Simon of Cyrene

10. The only "rationalistic" explanation for the resurrection widely promoted by scholars today is:

a) The vision and legendary-development theory
b) The swoon theory
c) The stolen body theory
d) The wrong tomb theory

Notes

www.ingramcontent.com/pod-product-compliance
Lightning Source LLC
Chambersburg PA
CBHW010920040426
42445CB00017B/1932